THE WORLD FOLKTALE LIBRARY

Tales from Africa

Tales from Africa

Selected and Retold by Lila Green

Illustrated by Jerry Pinkney

Consultants

Moritz A. Jagendorf
Author and Folklorist

Carolyn W. Field
Coordinator of Work with Children
The Free Library of Philadelphia

SILVER BURDETT COMPANY

Morristown, New Jersey
Glenview, Ill. • Palo Alto • Dallas • Atlanta

ISBN 0-382-03350-7

Library of Congress Catalog Card Number: 78-54623

INTRODUCTION

Folktales are old, easy to remember, and fun to listen to and tell. They may come from unfamiliar people and different parts of the world, but there is something in each one that you will recognize and understand. Most folktales are stories that were told and retold long before the invention of books and printing. That is how they got their name. They were passed along by word of mouth—one folk told another folk. Parents told their children. Neighbor shared with neighbor. Village folk told stories to entertain guests and travelers, who carried them to other parts of the world.

These folktales were gathered from all over the continent of Africa where there are many different peoples and ways of life. From each story, you will learn something important about the values and the lives of the people who tell it. Even as you laugh at Kasilo, the spider, you are learning how one culture views death and mourning. And in the story called "The Ungrateful Man," you will discover how another society feels about kindness and gratitude.

In Africa, folktales are a very important part of everyday life. People learn from them in very much the same way that you learn from history books, or from poems and stories about past times and people, such as Pocahontas and Paul Revere. When young people in Ghana hear about the ungrateful man, they, like you, learn some of the rules of their society.

THE EDITOR

Table of Contents

WHY SPIDERS HIDE IN CORNERS

This story is one of many spider tales from West Africa. In Sierra Leone, where the story takes place, it is believed that on the third day of mourning the spirit of the dead one "crosses the river."

One day, a messenger came from a distant village to the home of Kasilo the spider. He came to tell Kasilo that his mother-in-law had died. "Ndisah," Kasilo said to his wife, "you hurry ahead to prepare for your mother's funeral. I will come later." So Ndisah set off quickly for her mother's village.

When Kasilo was alone, he thought, "How can I show everyone that I am the biggest mourner of all?" Then he decided, "I will weep more than anyone else.

"I'll also fast for three days, until the spirit of my mother-in-law has crossed the river!"

As told to Lila Green by Lt. Col. Ambrose Patrick Genda, Sierra Leone Regiment.

He thought a little more. "I think I'll eat before I go."

And so Kasilo ate a very large meal, and then set off for his mother-in-law's village.

Kasilo saw that all his friends—Snake, Dog, Goat, Rabbit, and many more—were at the funeral. His wife's relatives were also there. Kasilo wept louder than anyone else. After the funeral, when everyone sat together and ate, Kasilo refused to eat, saying, "How can I eat when I am grieving so much for my mother-in-law? I will not eat until she has crossed the river.'' All the friends and relatives were surprised, for mourners are not expected to fast.

Twice that day Kasilo refused to eat. And on the second day, again he refused to eat. But all around him everyone else was eating. They were eating delicious foods prepared by the relatives. They were eating the gifts of food that people brought. Each had its own delicious aroma. Kasilo was very hungry, but he wanted to be called the greatest mourner of them all.

Later that day he went for a walk. As he passed a house in the village, he saw a pot of green bananas cooking over a fire. Nobody was near. Kasilo walked round and round the pot, breathing deeply. He looked in the pot and saw the bananas bobbing up and down in the boiling water. Near the pot was a bowl, and Kasilo took it and quickly filled it with a few of the bananas.

''Nobody will know if I eat just a few bananas,'' he said. He peeled one and popped it into his mouth. Just then some of his friends came into view. Down went the hot banana in one swallow. ''How can I save the rest of these bananas?'' he asked himself. Quickly, he tossed them into his hat, and quickly he put his hat on his head. But the hot banana did not go down well, and it burned in his chest. The bananas in his hat were scalding on the top of his head.

The creatures stared. "You don't look well," they said. "You have been fasting too long. You must eat now."

Kasilo thumped his chest where the banana burned inside. "No! No one is mourning more than I. I will not eat!"

The bananas in his hat were burning his head terribly. He shook his hat back and forth to move them. With the other hand, he thumped his chest.

"What is the matter, Kasilo?" asked the creatures.

Kasilo could barely keep still. He said, "There is a hat-shaking dance in my village now. I am shaking my hat as they do in my village."

"He has been fasting too long," said his friends. "That is why he is behaving so strangely. Come, Kasilo, come back and eat something."

"No," said Kasilo, dancing and thumping and shaking his hat. "No, they are shaking their hats in my village. They are dancing like this. They are calling me to join the dance. I must go to my village."

"Oh," said his friends, "surely you must eat before you leave."

"No! No!" Kasilo cried. But at that moment the pain became too great. He pulled his hat from his head, and all the bananas fell to the ground.

Everyone saw. They hooted and laughed. Kasilo was shamed. He ran into a house and looked for a place to hide. At last he climbed far into the corner of a ceiling.

Kasilo was driven to the ceiling by shame. To this day you may find him there. His head is bald, for the bananas burned off his hair. And all this happened because he tried to show off at his mother-in-law's funeral.

THE UNGRATEFUL MAN

This story comes from Ghana.

One day a very poor hunter was searching for food in the forest. He came to a very deep pit—dug to trap animals—and saw a strange sight: at the bottom were trapped a rat, a snake, a leopard, and a man. Each begged the hunter to help him escape.

The hunter was very kindhearted and he wished to help the creatures, but he was afraid the animals might do harm if they were freed. So he helped the man climb out, but he left the animals.

"Leopard," he said, "you steal people's cows!

"Snake, you bite people and kill them!

"Rat, you destroy people's property!

"It's best if all three of you stay where you are!"

But the animals pleaded hard for their lives. And

Adapted from "The Ungrateful Man" in *West African Folk Tales,* collected by W. H. Barker and Cecilia Sinclair. Copyright 1917 by George G. Harrap & Company Limited. Used by permission.

the kindhearted hunter finally gave in and helped them out of the pit.

"Thank you!" said the leopard, "I promise to repay this kindness."

The snake said the same thing, and so did the rat. Only the man said nothing. He seemed tired and terribly poor, so the hunter took him home and told him, "you are welcome to stay with me."

Soon the leopard came to the house. He brought much meat. "This will last you many weeks," he said. "Trade some of it for the things you need."

"Thank you," said the hunter.

A few days later the rat came to visit. He brought gold dust and ivory. "Sell these things, and they will make you rich," he told the hunter.

In a week or so the snake also came to visit. "I have something with which to repay you," he said. "It is a powder to be used against snake poison. Keep it carefully, for you may need it one day!" And the snake told him to mix the blood of a traitor with the powder when he needed to use it.

After the animals' visits, the hunter lived in great comfort. He had a comfortable house and all the things he needed. And he shared all these things with the man he had saved from the pit.

But this man had an envious nature. He was not content with sharing the hunter's good luck—he wanted to have everything for himself. He came to hate the kind hunter, and his thoughts became very spiteful.

One day, they heard that robbers had looted the King's palace. All of his jewels and gold were gone. The King was furious. He wanted his treasures back. So he promised a reward for the capture of the thieves.

The ungrateful man rushed to the palace. "What is the reward?" he asked the King. "If I can name the thief, what will you pay?"

"I'll give half of the stolen goods," said the King.

"The hunter is the thief!" cried the man. And he described the hunter's new riches and his sudden prosperity. The King sent for the hunter.

The honest hunter was brought before the King's judges. "Explain how you've grown so rich!" they demanded.

So the hunter told his story. He described how he had rescued the captives and how the animals had repaid him. But the judges would not believe him. They condemned him to die the following noon, for in olden times the penalty for stealing was death.

The next morning,while the hunter was wondering what might happen to save him, he heard a great commotion.

The King's son had been bitten by a snake and was dying of its poison.

"If anyone can cure my son," cried the King, "let him come quickly!"

The hunter called one of the guards. "Ask the King to let me try. I can cure his son with the powder the snake gave me."

The King was desperate, so he gave the hunter permission to try. And when the hunter explained he needed the blood of a traitor, the King ordered the ungrateful man beheaded, saying to the hunter, "He is a traitor! You saved his life and gave him shelter, and he turned you in!"

Then the hunter mixed the powder and applied it to the Prince's wound. In a moment the young Prince was well again.

The King was overjoyed. He loaded the hunter with many honors and sent him home.

THE WISE JUDGE

This is a humorous tale of justice from Ethiopia.

The widow Yemswitch was a good old woman, but she had long since grown hard of hearing. She had a small flock of sheep that she tended, and one day the sheep wandered off. Setting out to look for them, she met Farmer Mulugeta, who had just finished his plowing.

"Ato Mulugeta," said the widow, "have you seen my sheep today?"

Now Farmer Mulugeta was a good old man, but he too had grown hard of hearing. Since he had just come from his field, he thought she was asking about his plowing.

"Yes, Wizero Yemswitch," he answered, "I have worked very hard today." He pointed toward his plowed field to show her what he had done.

Abridged and simplified from *The Lion's Whiskers*, by Russell G. Davis and Brent K. Ashabranner, by permission of Little, Brown and Company. Copyright ©, 1959, by Russell G. Davis and Brent K. Ashabranner.

The widow had not heard a word. She thought he was pointing toward her lost flock of sheep.

"Thank you, Farmer Mulugeta," she said. "If I find them there, I shall give you one."

They bowed politely to each other. Then the widow went looking where the farmer had pointed. As luck would have it, she found the sheep just over the hill. She was grateful to the farmer for noting so carefully the way they had gone. In a little while, they might have been found by leopards or jackals.

The widow discovered that one of the lambs had an injured leg. She decided to give this lamb to the farmer. Going to his house, she found him preparing his supper, for his wife had been dead for many years.

"Ato Mulugeta," she said, "I found my sheep where you said they were. I've brought you this lamb for your reward."

Mulugeta did not hear a word, but he saw that the lamb had an injured leg. He thought the widow Yemswitch was accusing him of causing the injury.

"Oh, no," said the farmer. "I had nothing to do with it. Why should I want to hurt your lamb?"

The widow heard only the word "no." She thought

Mulugeta wanted a better sheep. "You are a greedy man," she said. "All you did was point the direction. Take this lamb, or you'll get none at all."

She tried to put the lamb in his arms, but he refused it. "I will not pay for this lamb," he said. "I had nothing to do with its injury."

They began to argue and say foolish things. This made little difference, of course, since neither could hear what the other was saying. But they made so much noise that at last a policeman came by. He insisted that they go to a judge to settle their quarrel.

They went to the court of an old and wise judge. This judge, Justice Yasu, was famous throughout the land for his fairness. Although he was wise, he was almost deaf. In addition to being deaf, he was almost blind. Thus, he could not judge people by the way they looked. And he could not judge them by the way they sounded. This made him a very fair judge.

The widow Yemswitch told her story first. Then pointing to the lamb, she said, "My reward is generous. Ato Mulugeta is a greedy man to want more."

Mulugeta then explained patiently that he was a kind man, who would never hurt a little lamb. "I was busy in my field," he said. "I had not even seen the lamb. But she brought it to my house and blamed me for its injured leg."

Justice Yasu listened carefully, but he couldn't

catch a word. For some time, he peered at the farmer and the widow. At last he made out that they were an old man and an old woman. The lamb in the woman's arms, he decided, was a child. Having had experience with people's troubles, the judge decided that this man and woman wanted a divorce. They

wanted him to say which one should keep the child.

"How many years have you been married?" asked the judge.

The widow listened carefully, but she only heard the words "how many." She thought the judge had asked how many sheep she owned.

"Twenty, Your Honor," she shouted loudly.

The judge heard this answer, and reached his decision. He said, "I'm ashamed of you both! You've been married twenty years and still have not learned to live together. You must go back and try harder. You must make a good home for your little child. If you do not, I shall put you both in prison. That is all. This case is dismissed!"

Neither the farmer nor the widow could hear him, but at last the bailiff made them understand the judge's decision.

"Make a home together?" cried the widow. "But we are not married!"

"Then get married at once," said the bailiff. "If you don't obey the judge's order, he will surely put you in prison."

And so the widow and the farmer went to a priest and were married that night.

Since she was a very good cook and he was a very good farmer—and since neither of them could hear the other—they lived happily ever after.

And wise Judge Yasu became still more famous throughout the land.

MUGASSA'S FEAST

A clever, mischievous rabbit is a familiar figure in many folk tales. This is a story of Rabbit in Uganda.

One day, Rabbit packed up a bundle of cloth that he wanted to trade for a cow. Then he set off for a village where people raised cows.

When he got there, instead of telling his business, he talked about other things. He gossiped with the women and joked with the men. People liked him. When he mentioned the trade, they accepted his cloth and gave him a cow.

Rabbit thanked the people politely and started home. It was getting dark when he reached the trail. "This is a place to meet trouble," thought Rabbit. "But if I run I'll lose my cow! So, if anything happens, instead of running away I'll stay still and use my head."

From *My Dark Companions*, by Henry M. Stanley, London, 1893, Sampson, Low, Marston and Company, Ltd.

Before long a lion sprang up and blocked Rabbit's way. "Hello there, Rabbit," he growled. "Where are you taking that cow?"

"Why, Lion," said Rabbit quickly, "I'm taking it to Mugassa. He is giving a feast. Don't you know you've been invited?"

Since Mugassa was a god, Lion was pleased. "That is a great honor," he said. "So, if you don't mind, Rabbit, I'll walk along behind you."

Rabbit and Lion had not gone far before an ugly buffalo jumped toward them.

"You! Rabbit! Where are you taking that cow?" he asked fiercely.

"I'm driving the cow to Mugassa," said Rabbit. "And since you've been invited to his feast, you may come along with us!"

"Ah, that's good news," answered Buffalo, feeling important. "I'm lucky I met you!" And Buffalo took his place behind Lion.

Soon they met a bad-tempered elephant, who stood in the middle of the road and trumpeted, "Rabbit! Where are you taking that cow?"

"Now, Elephant," said Rabbit, "get out of the way. We're taking the cow to Mugassa, and he will be angry if we're late. Haven't you heard about his feast?"

"Is Mugassa giving a feast?" asked Elephant.

"Yes," replied Rabbit. "And since you are one of the guests, you may help drive this cow. I'll ride on your back. I'm getting awfully tired!"

"Certainly," said Elephant happily, "I'll carry you with pleasure." So Rabbit hopped up on Elephant's back.

Then a leopard and a hyena jumped out and snarled. But seeing the powerful crowd, they were very polite, and both were invited to come along.

It was dark when they all came to Rabbit's village. They were met at the gates by two dogs, and Rabbit jumped down and greeted them. He whispered to the dogs what had happened, and they wagged their tails and laughed. Then one ran into the village. When he returned, he pretended to whisper a message from Mugassa in Rabbit's ear.

Then Rabbit said in an important voice, "Mugassa says the cow is to be killed. The meat is to be cleaned and laid on mats. When this is done,

Mugassa will come and cook with you. He says you are all very welcome.

"You, Hyena, must kill the cow and clean the meat. But remember—don't eat any! If the meat is touched before Mugassa comes, he will be very angry.

"Buffalo, you must find dead wood for the fire and bring it to Elephant. Remember, it must have smooth bark.

"Elephant, you must chop the wood, but be sure to take care of the hatchet—it belongs to Mugassa!

"Leopard," continued Rabbit, "you must find a banana tree and catch falling leaves. We will use them for plates.

"Lion, my friend, you must take this pot to the spring and fill it. We will need it for cooking vegetables."

Having given his orders, Rabbit ran off in the grass. He hid himself well and watched to see what would happen.

Buffalo found a log with smooth bark. The dogs barked, "That's not enough!" And they sent him back to find some more.

Elephant took the log and began to chop it. But

the hatchet broke at the first blow. Now there was nothing for chopping the wood.

Leopard found a banana tree. He watched for leaves, but leaves didn't fall.

Lion's pot had a hole in the bottom. Though he tried and tried, he could never fill it.

In the meantime, Hyena killed the cow and he cleaned the meat. "Now," he said to the dogs, "what shall I do with it?"

"Help us carry it into the village and put it on mats," said the dogs. "But don't eat any!"

Hyena looked unhappy. "It looks so nice and fat," he said, "and I'm so terribly hungry. See how my mouth is watering? Let's eat just a little."

"Oh, no!" said the dogs. "We would all be ruined! Have patience! We haven't long to wait."

Hyena agreed, but he managed to hide a piece in the grass. Rabbit saw everything, but he said nothing.

When all the meat had been carried in, Hyena went back to find his meat. Quietly, he lay down in the grass to enjoy it. But before he could take the first bite, Rabbit called, "Hyena is a thief! I see you! Stop, thief! Mugassa is coming!" Hyena became so frightened that he dropped the meat and ran.

The others—Buffalo, Elephant, Lion, and Leopard —were deeply ashamed of their work. They heard Rabbit shout and they saw Hyena run away. "Mugassa is angry," they said. "Let us run for our lives." And soon they were lost in the jungle.

Rabbit and the dogs returned to the village. They closed the gate and locked it. All night long they feasted. They had the entire feast to themselves, and every time they thought of their trick, they rolled on the ground with laughter.

But Rabbit laughed loudest of all, for he was the smartest.

HAMDANI

This story comes from the part of Tanzania that is called Zanzibar.

There was once a poor man named Hamdani. He begged from door to door for his food, and sometimes he begged for people's old clothes. Finally people grew tired of him, and no one bothered to answer his knock.

Times grew harder for Hamdani. Each day, he went to the villagers' dust heap and gathered the leftover grains of millet. These he would cook to make a hard cereal.

One day, as he hunted for millet, he found a small coin. A peddler with a cage was passing, and Hamdani called to him, "Peddler, what do you carry there?"

"Gazelles," said the peddler.

From *Zanzibar Tales*, by G. W. Bateman, Chicago, 1901, A. C. McClurg and Company.

"Please bring them here and let me see them."

"Certainly! Right away!" said the peddler.

Some men who were passing by laughed and said, "Don't waste your time on him, my good man! He's poorer than you are!"

"Richer ones waste my time!" said the peddler. "I go to anyone who calls me!" Shrugging, he made his way to the dust heap.

Hamdani peered into the cage. "May I buy a small gazelle with this coin?"

"That isn't much money! But you may have this small one—it is named Kijipah." The peddler took out the smallest gazelle and went on his way.

Hamdani stayed at the dust heap and hunted for millet. At sundown he took the gazelle to his hut.

Each day they did the same. To the dust heap they went in the morning; home they went in the evening. Hamdani was happy now. He had company and someone to look after.

One night Hamdani was startled to hear the gazelle call.

"Master, master!"

"Who is it?" asked Hamdani.

"Your gazelle," said Kijipah. "I am starving to

death. Just let me hunt on my own, I'll return to the hut every evening."

The thought of losing the gazelle made Hamdani sad. But what could he do?

It was dawn as he watched Kijipah run from the hut. Tears came to his eyes. He ran outdoors, and cried to the air, "My gazelle is gone! My gazelle is gone!"

"Fool!" called a neighbor. "You bought a gazelle when you might have bought food! Now it has gone! It's your own fault—so don't disturb us."

Hamdani was sadder than ever.

But that evening, Kijipah came back. "Have you really come back?" asked Hamdani joyfully.

"Of course," said Kijipah and stretched out on his mat. He told Hamdani about the places he had been and the foods he had eaten.

From then on, every day Hamdani went to the dust heap and Kijipah went hunting. In the evenings they met at home and talked.

Then one day while hunting in the forest, the gazelle found a diamond! It was the largest one he had ever seen.

"This is worth a kingdom!" exclaimed the gazelle.

"But I can't bring it home! People will think my master stole it, and he will be killed. Still, this diamond will bring us luck!"

Kijipah wrapped the stone in leaves, and taking it in his mouth, he ran through the forest. For three days he ran without rest, until he came to a city. There he followed the main street, right to the Sultan's palace.

The Sultan was sitting at the door of his palace, so Kijipah approached and greeted him humbly. His Majesty was astonished at the talking gazelle. He ordered food, and a carpet for Kijipah to rest on. "Now," said the Sultan, "what news do you bring me?"

"Your Majesty, I come from my master, the Sultan Darahi, but perhaps you will not be pleased with his message." Kijipah knelt at the Sultan's feet.

"What is his message?" asked the Sultan.

"Sultan Darahi wishes to bring the royal families closer. He proposes to marry your daughter. This small stone he sends you, to pledge his intentions." Kijipah dropped the diamond on the Sultan's lap.

The Sultan was greatly impressed. Only another fabulous Sultan could own such a diamond—and such a gazelle! "Your master has my consent," he said. "Let him come as soon as he can!"

Meanwhile the beggar was in despair over Kijipah. Neglecting the dust heap, he crept through the streets moaning, "My poor gazelle! My poor gazelle!" His neighbors jeered and taunted him until he was nearly out of his mind.

One evening, Kijipah finally appeared. The beggar hugged him and asked where he had been. But Kijipah only said, "Master, get some sleep. Tomorrow we must begin a long journey."

At dawn they set off through the forest and they walked for four days. On the fifth day, they stopped at a stream. "Master, stay here," said Kijipah, "and don't leave this stream. I'll be back very soon." Leaving the beggar, he ran to the Sultan's palace.

Soldiers, who were posted along the road, were surprised to see the gazelle alone. They escorted him to the Sultan.

"What news do you bring?" asked the Sultan.

"Bad news!" replied the gazelle. "My master met up with a band of robbers. They tied him up and took everything—even his clothes!"

Quickly the Sultan sent for new clothing: a long, white robe and a black overjacket; a band for the waist, and a turban; a gold-hilted sword and a curved dagger; and last, a pair of new sandals. The soldiers fastened the clothes on a horse.

"These soldiers will go with you," said the Sultan.

But Kijipah said, "My master would not want to be seen now. I will take the things myself." Taking the lead-rope in his mouth he set off with the horse, to the great admiration of all.

When he returned to Hamdani, Kijipah led him to the stream. "Come, Master, get in and bathe yourself!" he said.

Hamdani rubbed his teeth clean with sand, bathed, and washed his hair.

Soon he was very much changed. "Now put on these clothes," said Kijipah.

At last, wearing the fine clothes, Hamdani mounted the Sultan's horse. Taking the rope, Kijipah led the way.

Halfway to the city, Kijipah stopped. "Master, today you're a new man. No one would know you've been in the dust heap. Even your neighbors would never suspect it.

"Now we're on our way to a very large city. The Sultan of the city expects you to marry his daughter. But your speech may give you away, so let me do the talking!"

"I'll do as you say," said Hamdani.

"And, master, remember!—You are the Sultan of Darahi!"

They were soon met by soldiers, who escorted them to the city. The Sultan and other great men were waiting when they arrived. The two Sultans bowed deeply to each other and walked to the palace together. A great feast was waiting. All that day, and all that night, the court celebrated. The next day Hamdani married the Sultan's daughter.

For many days the festivities lasted, but then Kijipah had to leave. "I must return home and put things in order," he said to the Sultan. To Hamdani, he said, "Stay here, Master—don't leave until I return."

Kijipah began his journey but soon came to a very fine town. He was astonished to see that it was deserted.

At the end of one street was the biggest house he had ever seen. It was built of turquoise, sapphire, and the most precious stones. "This is just the house for a Sultan! My master would do very well here," he thought.

He knocked at the door and called, "Hello! Hello there! Is anyone home?"

An old woman opened the door and whispered, "The Great Snake With Seven Heads lives here. All the townspeople have run away from him! You'd best go away before he comes back!"

Just then the Great Snake appeared. Its first head came quickly in the door, then the second. But Kijipah moved even faster. Taking a huge sword from the wall he chopped off the two heads. Then, moving like lightning, he cut off the other five heads.

"That's the end of that snake!" said Kijipah.

The old woman was overjoyed! She told him the house was now his. There were storerooms full of silks and jewels, chambers full of servants, and stables full of the very best horses.

Kijipah said to the woman, "Take care of these things. They are for my master, Sultan Darahi." And he set off for the Sultan's palace.

Everyone there was happy to see the gazelle again. For a few days, Kijipah visited with his friends. Then he said, "Master, you can take your bride home now. I will tell the Sultan that you are ready."

The following day a great crowd gathered to ride with the pair. There were horsemen, and servants, and ladies-in-waiting, and Kijipah led them all. The trip took three days, and on the fourth day they arrived at Hamdani's new home. Seeing the gazelle, the old woman came down and hugged him and kissed his feet.

"No, no, Grandmother!" said Kijipah. "You must give first honors to Sultan Darahi!"

So the old woman kissed the feet of the new Sultan, and led the guests to their rooms. Soon there was feasting and laughing in the house.

Weeks passed, and the guests returned to their city. Hamdani and his bride enjoyed living in the splendid house. But Hamdani was changing. He no longer remembered the gazelle who had brought him good fortune. "Why fuss about a gazelle that I bought for a coin!" he thought.

One day Kijipah said to the old woman, "I'm very sad, Grandmother, I don't understand my master. I killed the snake and got this house for him, yet he doesn't even speak to me."

For many days Kijipah barely ate. One morning the old woman heard him moaning. "Tell my master I am ill," Kijipah whispered to her.

The old woman went upstairs. She found the master and the mistress sitting on their marble

couch. "What do you want?" asked Hamdani.

"Master," she said, "Kijipah is ill."

"Oh!" said Hamdani's wife, in alarm. "What is the matter?"

"He aches all over—he's very feverish and hasn't eaten."

But Hamdani only said, "Well, why bother us?

Give him some of the red millet that we won't eat."

His wife was amazed. "Can't we give him something better than millet?" she asked.

"You talk too much," said Hamdani. "It's good enough for a gazelle that I bought for a coin."

The old woman cooked the millet, and wept for Kijipah. "Did he tell you to give me that?" asked the gazelle.

"Yes," said the woman.

"Well," said Kijipah, "give him one more chance. Go back and say that I am very ill. Ask him to send for a doctor."

Again the old woman went upstairs. The master and the mistress were drinking coffee. "What's the matter now?" asked Hamdani gruffly.

"Kijipah is very ill," she said. "He can't eat the millet, and he asks . . ."

"Oh, bother what he asks!" exclaimed Hamdani. "Close your ears, and don't listen! Pay no attention at all!"

Tears filled the eyes of Hamdani's wife.

"What's the matter, Sultan's daughter?"

"I'm sorry for Kijipah!" she said.

"You've lost your senses!" he exclaimed.

"But the people love him dearly!" she said. "They will blame you for neglecting him. Be kind to him. He has brought you everything you have!"

Hamdani raised his voice. "How dare you talk to me that way! You've lost your wits. You should be put in chains!"

Turning to the old woman, he said, "Tell that gazelle he's only a creature I bought for a coin! I'm not to be bothered with more of his messages!"

Hamdani's wife hurried out. She sent for her father's doctor, but he came too late. Kijipah was dead.

"Throw him into the well!" said Hamdani. The servants had no choice but to do it.

When the people saw this, they stood in the courtyard and wept.

"What is this fuss about?" shouted Hamdani. "You are weeping as if I had died! Stop this, all of you!"

Hamdani's wife could not stop weeping. When darkness fell, she sent the servants to bury Kijipah. Then she went to bed and had a dream. She dreamed she was back at her father's house, and when she awoke she found it was true. She was home with her people around her. And there she lived happily all of her life.

Hamdani, too, had a dream. He dreamed he was back at his dust heap, dressed in his rags. When he awoke, there he was, his hands full of dust. He stared about wildly, shaking his head. Then he saw children he knew. "Ha, ha, Hamdani!" they laughed. "Where have you been? Have you found much millet today?"

To the end of his days, he stayed at the dust heap, hunting for millet to keep himself alive.

MINU

This is a story from Ghana.

One day a man from a small village in Ghana set out for the city of Accra. He had some business there. The city was far and the people used a different language. But the traveler didn't know this.

He traveled for days. Finally he came to the edge of the city. There he saw a great herd of cows. "I have never seen such plenty and wealth," he thought. "Could this all belong to one man?" Seeing a farmer, he stopped to ask. "To whom do these cows belong?" he said.

The farmer did not understand. His language was different. "Minu," he said, which means *I don't understand*. The traveler did not understand either.

"Ah, Mr. Minu must be very rich!" thought the man.

He went on his way into the city.

On every side, he found wonderful shops. Stopping to stare at the largest one, he thought, "Who could possibly own it?"

Just then a man passed by, and the traveler asked him, "Whose shop is this?"

But the man did not understand. "Minu," he said.

"Mr. Minu? This, too, is his? He must be wealthy indeed," said the traveler.

Shaking his head in great wonder, the traveler walked on through the streets, passing many fine homes. "The homes of Accra are so grand—not at all like the huts of my village!" he said to himself.

Seeing a very fine house, he admired its size and the gardens around it. Just then a servant came out. "Please tell me," said the traveler, "who owns this house."

The servant shrugged. "Minu," she mumbled.

"Ah, what a silly question!" he said. "I should have known—the great Mr. Minu!" And the traveler went on.

He came to the harbor in Accra. Everything there caught his eye: the ships, the sailors, the ocean, the sky. Men were hurrying by him loading a great ship. "What a fine cargo!" he said. "If I owned even a small part of it, how rich I would be. I'd be as rich as the great Mr. Minu. I'd have a house, and shop, and cattle like his instead of a poor little hut!"

He turned to a bystander. "Who owns this ship and its cargo?" he asked. To his amazement, the answer was "Minu."

"Minu!" said the traveler. "Why, he's the wealthiest man in the world!"

Later that day, the traveler finished his business. Then he set out for home. As he walked down a street, he passed some men who were carrying a coffin. They were followed by a long procession, all dressed in black. "This is a very big funeral procession," thought the traveler. "Only an important person would have so many mourners at his funeral." Stopping one of the mourners, he asked, "Which esteemed citizen has passed away?"

But the mourner did not understand. "Minu," he said. Then he walked on.

"The great Minu is dead? That is bad news indeed!" said the traveler. "So . . . ! He had to leave all his business and wealth to die as any poor man would die! Well, I'll be content to live on in my hut."

And he went home, both healthy and happy.

THE RABBIT AND THE CLAY MAN

This is a West African story about the familiar figure Rabbit, who is similar to the American "Brer Rabbit."

Long ago in Africa there lived a rabbit named Wakaima. His best friend was an elephant named Wanjovu. Together they shared a house and a farm.

The elephant worked very hard on the farm, but Rabbit was very lazy, and seldom worked at all. At last the elephant grew tired of doing all the work. He said to the rabbit, "Wakaima, let us each have a separate farm. You will work on yours, and I will work on mine. Then we will share what we grow."

Rabbit agreed.

So they selected plots, prepared the soil, and planted the seed. The elephant worked hard on his farm, but the rabbit ran off each day to the jungle.

Adapted from "Wakaima and the Clay Man," in *Wakaima and the Clay Man, and Other African Folk Tales*, by E. Balintuma Kalibala and Mary Gould Davis. Copyright 1946 by Longmans, Green and Co. Reprinted by permission of the David McKay Company, Inc.

He ate wild fruit and spent his days loafing and sleeping. Each evening he rubbed dirt on his paws and returned to the house. Rubbing his back, he groaned about how hard he had worked and how tired he was.

The elephant believed him. He was sorry for his friend, and always cooked supper for him.

One evening as they sat down for supper, the elephant said, "Wakaima, I'm afraid that you are working too hard."

But the rabbit shook his head. "We must work harder than ever," he said. "The rains are coming, and we must have plenty of food to store away."

Things went on this way for weeks. At last the crops were ready, and the time had come to harvest them.

One evening, the elephant brought home a basket of corn and potatoes. He cooked them for himself and the rabbit.

"How good your corn is!" said Rabbit. "And I have never eaten better potatoes!"

The next evening, the rabbit brought home a basket of corn and potatoes. "These are not as good as yours," he apologized.

The elephant looked them over. They looked very much like his own. But he said nothing, and cooked them for supper.

The next day the elephant went to his farm. He saw that some corn and potatoes were gone, and he knew he himself had not picked them. That evening he said to the rabbit, "Someone got into my farm last night and stole some corn and potatoes!"

"Really?" said Rabbit. "Some thief got into my farm, too! What shall we do about it?" Of course he had stolen them all himself.

"We must keep him away," said the elephant. "I will think about it and work out a plan."

Next day the elephant went to the river. He dug a great deal of clay, and built a clay man. Then he carried it to his farm and set it between the potatoes and corn. By the time he was finished, night had fallen and the moon had risen.

The elephant returned to his house and went to bed. He was fast asleep when the rabbit stole out to the elephant's farm.

There stood the clay man, big in the moonlight. Rabbit was frightened. "Who is this?" he thought. "Can it be Wanjovu waiting to punish me? Does he suspect I have stolen his vegetables?"

He did not move. The clay man did not move. At last the rabbit found courage to speak. "Hullo, Wanjovu," he called. "What are you doing out here so late?"

The clay man did not answer.

Rabbit began to lose his temper. "You are not Wanjovu!" he shouted. "You are a thief who is stealing his corn! Tell me who you are, or I will go and get Wanjovu."

The clay man did not answer.

Rabbit was puzzled. He went a little closer. "Who are you? Why don't you say something?"

The clay man did not answer.

The rabbit walked all around the clay man. He looked very big in the moonlight. "Answer me," shouted Rabbit. "If you don't, I will hit you!"

But the clay man did not answer.

The rabbit went up to the clay man. He hit him with one of his paws. And there his paw stuck in the soft, wet clay.

"Let me go!" said Rabbit. "Let me go, or I will hit you with my other paw!"

But the clay man did not let him go.

The rabbit lifted his other paw and hit the clay man as hard as he could. His other paw stuck. He couldn't free it.

Furiously Rabbit shouted, "Let me go, I tell you! Let me go, or I will kick you!"

But the clay man did not let go.

The rabbit raised his foot and kicked him. His foot stuck fast in the soft, wet clay. He pulled hard and yelled at the clay man.

But the clay man would not let go.

So the rabbit lifted his other foot. He kicked the clay man with all his strength. His other foot stuck —he couldn't free it!

"I will bite you with my teeth!" screamed Rabbit. "Let me go, or I will bite you with my teeth!"

But the clay man held him fast.

The rabbit bit the clay man with his long sharp teeth. And they stuck in the clay.

Now the rabbit could not move. He could not speak. He could only wait for morning.

When the sun began to rise and the birds began to sing, the elephant woke up. He hurried to his farm to see if the clay man had trapped the thief.

And there, stuck in the clay, was Wakaima!

"You wicked creature!" he bellowed. "You are the one who has stolen my vegetables. I suppose it was easier to steal mine than to grow your own. Now I shall have to punish you!"

The elephant pulled the rabbit loose.

"What are you going to do?" sobbed Rabbit.

"I'm thinking about it," answered the elephant. But he began to feel a little sorry for the rabbit. "What would you do with a lazy, good-for-nothing, deceitful creature?" he asked.

"I would throw him into the jungle—high up in a tree," said Rabbit.

"Very well, that's what I'll do," said the elephant.

Elephant took Rabbit into the jungle, and there threw him high into the branches of a tree. But Rabbit landed safely on his feet and bounded off far into the jungle.

The elephant knew he could never catch him. He went back to his farm to tend his crops.

Since that day the elephant and the rabbit have never spoken to each other.

HOW ABUNAWAS WAS EXILED

This story comes from Ethiopia.

They say that long ago in Ethiopia there was a fellow named Abunawas, who was known everywhere for his cleverness.

It is told among the old people that one day Abunawas came to the town where the Negus, or Emperor lived. He went to the palace of the Negus and asked for work.

"You look like a strong man," the Negus said. "I will make you a guard."

So they gave Abunawas weapons, and he became a guard of the Negus' house.

One day the Negus called Abunawas and said: "I am going away. See that you watch the palace gate."

"I will watch it," Abunawas said.

From *The Fire on the Mountain* by Harold Courlander and Wolf Leslau. Copyright 1950 by Holt, Rinehart and Winston, Inc. Reprinted by permission of Holt, Rinehart and Winston, Inc.

The Negus and his party rode away. Abunawas sat at the gate and watched. He became lonesome. He heard dancing in the city. At last he said to himself:

"The Negus didn't say I wasn't to dance."

So he took the gate from its hinges and carried it to the place where people were dancing. There he spent the night singing and drinking, and when the sky grew light he returned to the Negus' house, still carrying the gate with him. But during his absence, thieves had come and looted the palace.

When the Negus returned he was angry, and he sent for Abunawas. He said:

"Weren't you entrusted with guarding my house?"

"Why," said Abunawas, "you told me only to watch the gate, and I didn't let it out of my sight. You said nothing about the palace."

"Ah, you of the clever tongue!" the Negus said. "Tomorrow you shall be punished!" He called his servants. "Take this man outside the palace grounds and hold him prisoner," he said.

The servants took Abunawas away, and outside the palace grounds they dug a hole and put him into it. Then they filled in the hole until only Abunawas' head was showing. After this, they went away.

Abunawas stood this way in the hole all night without being able to move hand or foot. When morning came, a merchant with a caravan of camels passed. The merchant stopped when he saw Abunawas.

"Peace be with you," the merchant said. "What are you doing down there?"

"To you also, peace," Abunawas said. "I am being straightened out."

"How is that?"

"Why, I had a crooked back, and the Negus' doctors buried me here yesterday to straighten it," Abunawas answered.

"How fortunate you are to know the Emperor's doctors," the merchant said. "I also have a crooked back, but I didn't know there was a cure."

"This is the cure," Abunawas said. "I feel straight as a spear."

"I would give anything to be in your place!" the merchant said.

"Would you give all your camels?" Abunawas asked.

"I would give *half* of my camels."

"Very well, we agree. Dig me out," Abunawas said.

The merchant dug Abunawas out of the hole, and he himself got into it. Abunawas packed the dirt tightly around him so that only his head was showing.

"I shall never forget your goodness," the merchant said.

"May you live to remember," Abunawas said. He took not half but all of the camels and went away.

Before long the Negus' servants came. Thinking the merchant was the same man they had buried, they took him out of the hole, dragged him back and forth across the sand, and beat him with sticks. All this time he was shouting:

"Stop, I am straight enough! Stop, I am straight enough!"

At last, puzzled by this strange talk, they took him to the Negus.

"Who is this man?" the Negus asked.

"Abunawas," they replied.

"No, I am not Abunawas!" the merchant cried,

and he told the Negus his story.

"Ah, that Abunawas is a clever fellow!" the Negus said. "But let us see how clever he is."

He turned to his messengers and said:

"Go everywhere and look for Abunawas. When you have found him, give him this message:

"The Negus commands you to come to him at once. But you must be neither naked nor clothed, and you must be neither walking nor riding."

The messengers went out and found Abunawas, and repeated the Negus' command:

"You must be neither naked nor clothed, and you must be neither walking nor riding."

Then they returned to the Negus and informed him they had found Abunawas. The news spread, and a crowd gathered before the Negus' house to witness how he had outwitted Abunawas.

"He comes!" someone shouted, and the people craned their necks to see. Suddenly Abunawas came into sight. A laugh went up and spread through the crowd. Abunawas had no clothes on, but a fish net was wrapped around him. He had one foot in the horse's stirrup and the other foot on the ground. As the horse advanced, Abunawas hopped along on one foot.

The Negus was crestfallen. When the crowd stopped laughing he spoke. He said:

"Abunawas, this is your last prank. You are clever, but you are a great nuisance. I will not punish you on one single condition: that I never see your face again!"

So Abunawas went away.

Some days later the Negus was riding through the city. As he came to the market place, everyone turned toward him and bowed. But in the crowd there was a man who stood with his back to the Negus.

The Emperor grew angry.

"Bring me the man who turns his back on me!" he said.

They went and took hold of the man and brought him to Negus. It was Abunawas.

"Ha, it is you! How dare you turn your back on the Negus?"

"Why, I merely followed your command," Abunawas said. "You told me never again to show you my face, so I turned my back."

"Your tongue is still clever, but you are insolent,"

the Negus said. "This is my last order to you. Leave Ethiopia at once. I do not care which way you go, but if you ever again set foot on Ethiopian earth I will hang you!"

Abunawas went away, and the people laughed for many days over how he had outwitted the Negus. But they also shook their heads over the penalty he had paid.

One day there was a festival in the city, and the streets were crowded with people from the countryside. The Negus rode out on his horse. And there, standing at the entrance to the market place was Abunawas.

The Negus rode forward and help up his hand for silence.

"People of Ethiopia," he said, "our festival has been spoiled for us, for I am obliged to hang a man." He turned to Abunawas. "I see you have forgotten my last words."

"No, I have remembered," Abunawas said. "You ordered me never again to set foot on Ethiopian soil."

"Then why are you here?"

"I have followed your instructions faithfully,"

Abunawas said. "I left Ethiopia, as you told me to do. I went to Egypt, and there I put earth in my shoes. And ever since that day I have walked only upon Egyptian soil."

THE PRINCE WHO WANTED THE MOON

This story is from the Congo. In some ways it resembles the European story "The Princess Who Wanted the Moon."

There once was a King of Bandimba who had many, many daughters. But he had no sons. Because of this he was very sad. He envied anyone at all who had such wealth as to have a son. He would say, "If a son is born to me, I shall grant him whatever he wishes."

At last the day came when a son was born to the King. He and all of Bandimba rejoiced.

As the young Prince grew into a strong and handsome boy, his father granted him all that he desired. But the Prince always forgot what he had, and wished for more.

One day the Prince boasted to his friends, "My

From *My Dark Companions*, by Henry M. Stanley, London, 1893, Sampson, Low, Marston and Company, Ltd.

father loves me very much. He loves me so much that there is nothing he will not give me."

All the boys agreed, except the smallest one. "It's true," he said. "Your father loves you, and he is generous. But there is something he will never give you."

"The King will give me anything!" said the Prince angrily.

"Well," replied the boy, "he can't give you the moon."

"Do you think not?" asked the Prince. "I will ask my father for it!" He hurried to the palace.

"Father," he said, "my friend says that you will not give me the moon, and I want it more than anything else."

"The moon is a long way up, my child. How would we ever reach it?"

"I don't know, Father, but I am sure you will be able to get it for me."

"I don't think we can give you the moon," said the King.

"But I must have it, Father! I told my friends you would give it to me! If I don't have the moon, I will surely die."

"Don't speak of death, my Prince," said the King. "Don't you know that I live only for you? I will ask the wise men's advice. If they say that the moon can be reached, you shall have it."

The state drum was sounded, and all the wise men came together to the palace.

"I want to know if the moon can be reached," said the King. "I want to give it to my son. If one of you knows how to do it, I will give you my favorite daughter in marriage. Indeed, I will make you rich for your lifetime."

When the wise men heard this request, they were speechless. They looked at one another. "The King has gone mad!" they seemed to be saying. But the youngest of the wise men stood up.

"If the King will assist me, I will bring the moon down," he said.

All faces turned toward the man. "How will you do it?" asked the King.

"I will build a great tower on top of the mountain. On this tower, I will build a taller tower. On the second, I will build a third, on the third, a fourth, and so on, until my shoulders touch the moon."

"It can be reached this way?" asked the King.

"It can," said the man. "But it will take an army of workmen and forests of timber."

"You shall have them," said the King. "Each man in the kingdom will be at your service."

"That's not enough," said the man. "We'll need the women and children, too. The men will cut trees and square timber. The women will cook for the workmen. The boys will make bark rope. And all the girls will raise cassava roots for food."

"Let it be as you say," said the King. "The people are placed at your service."

So the people of Bandimba gathered together and began working. The forest was cut down, and the timbers were squared. Holes were dug for the base of the tower. Rope coils were made of bark and of palm fiber. Endless loaves of bread were baked; vegetables and green bananas were cooked. The fields were hoed, and corn was planted. Cassavas and plantains were grown.

The Bandimba people worked day and night to build the tower.

In two months, the tower reached the sky. Still the men kept building.

From all the countries around, people came to

watch. "The Bandimba have gone mad," they said, but they admired the tower just the same.

After six months, the engineer sent word he was reaching the moon.

"Excellent," said the King. "I will come up now." Twenty days later he reached the top of the tower and stood near the moon. "How will you move it?" he asked.

"I will put it on my shoulders and carry it down." The engineer put his shoulders beneath the moon. But the moon stood firm. However hard the engineer pushed, he couldn't budge it. He pushed harder and harder, until suddenly it cracked open.

The explosion was heard all over the earth. Fire and sparks rained down on the platform. Hot melted rock flowed down through the tower. A large piece of the moon then fell burning to the earth, and a river of fire ran over the land.

No one from the country of Bandimba is left. The foolish King and his greedy Prince brought ruin to themselves and their land, and the country was

turned into ashes and dust.

But you can still see the dark spots of the moon, where the engineer's shoulders bumped.

DIGIT THE MIDGET

This tale comes from the highland people of Ethiopia.

A woman of Munz had seven large, strong, stupid sons. They went about the house breaking chairs with their weight. They emptied the *injera* basket and the *wot* pot with their great appetites. They filled the house with the terrifying rumble of their snoring. And although they were very strong, they were lazy and would not work. They just ate, slept, snored, and got in the way of their patient and hardworking mother.

One day this poor woman could stand her house and clumsy family no longer and ran away to the shore of Lake Haik.

There she knelt down and cried in a loud voice, "Oh Allah and all Your Angels and Saints, hear my prayer. I have been sent seven of the biggest, clumsiest and laziest sons in all of Ethiopia. Soon I am to have another child. I would like a clever daughter. But if You don't send me a daughter, please send me a very small son."

Now Allah hears all prayers, but answers only some. He did not send a daughter. But He did send a very tiny son. The son was named Digit. He was only half the length of a man's thumb. The woman was delighted with her new child. Digit was the first of her children that she had ever been able to carry in her arms. She had had to hire a mule to bring each of her other sons home.

In the days to come, the mother grew even happier. While her huge sons grew bigger and bigger, Digit did not grow at all. What's more, he seemed to be a clever boy.

Because Digit was so small, he had to be clever. He often had to save himself from being crushed to death by his huge and clumsy brothers.

One night, the house door was left open. Digit was blown out into the yard by the wind of his brothers' snoring. Before the dawn came, he was nearly eaten by a chicken and carried off by a mouse. After that, Digit's mother tried never to let him out of her sight and reach.

As the years passed, the seven huge brothers came to hate Digit. They were very jealous. When they had been babies, their mother had never taken them on her lap. She had never kissed them on the top of their heads. She had never even seen the tops of their heads.

She never hugged them, because her arms would

not fit around them. They could not hug her, because once the eldest had tried and had broken three of her ribs.

It was clear that Digit was her favorite. She always took the choicest meat from the wot for him. She made the huge brothers crack the bones and pick the marrow out for Digit.

The brothers complained, "Mama doesn't hug and kiss us. She never calls us her little stalks of sugar. Never! With that little fiend gone, Mama would love us again." The brothers plotted and schemed to get rid of Digit.

They made life so hard for Digit that he moved out of the house to his own little house. And Mama then was so angry that she made the brothers leave home too.

One night the brothers came and burned Digit's house. But Digit was clever and saved himself. He slipped through a hole in the floor into the tunnel of a rabbit. He walked through the tunnel to safety.

The next morning Digit loaded the ashes of his house into sacks and had the sacks loaded onto mules. He decided to leave town to escape his brothers.

The first night, Digit stopped at the house of a rich man. In the morning, he looked into his sacks and began to scream, "Robbery! Thief! Some thief took my flour and filled the sacks with ashes."

Digit screamed and screamed. The rich man felt sorry for the poor little boy. He did not want his neighbors to think he would steal flour from a midget, so he gave Digit seven sacks of flour. And Digit decided to return home and give the flour to his mother.

When he returned, Digit told his brothers how he had tricked the rich man. "A very clever trick," all the brothers agreed. They went to their own houses, burned them down, and loaded the ashes onto mules.

The first brother went to the home of the rich man and spent the night. When he opened his sacks in the morning, he screamed that he had been robbed— just as Digit had done. But the rich man ordered him out of the house. When the second brother came along the next day, and tried the same trick, the rich man had his servants throw him into the road. When the third brother arrived, the rich man had him beaten with sticks.

The fourth brother arrived, and the rich man

asked, "What do you have in those sacks?"

"Flour," replied the stupid brother.

"Good," said the rich man, "we are short of flour. We'll make your bread tonight from your flour."

That night the stupid brother had to eat ashes bread, and the next morning he was driven from the

rich man's home.

The rich man played the same trick on the fifth and sixth brothers. Finally, when the seventh brother came by, the rich man was tired of his own joke. He turned the dogs loose on that one.

The angry brothers gathered around the bed of

the seventh brother. "Digit must go!" they decided.

One night, while their mother slept, the brothers took Digit. They pushed him into an injera basket, tied down the lid, and threw the basket into the river. They were sure that they would never see Digit the Midget again.

But the current carried the basket and washed it up on the shore. In the morning, an Arab merchant named Yusef found the basket. He opened it, and out hopped Digit. Digit danced and sang, "Oh, you are lucky. You are Allah's favored son."

"Why am I lucky?" said Yusef. "I have only found a wet little boy on a riverbank. What is so lucky about that?"

"Do I look unusual, or strange?" asked Digit.

"You are unusually small," replied Yusef.

"Yes," said Digit, "I am very small. It is because I am the messenger of Allah. I could not fit into this magic basket if I were not so small. And what a magic basket it is! Each day, at noon, it fills with gold."

Yusef was greedy. He wanted to keep the magic basket. But he was also worried. He said, "If I took the magic basket into town, the governor would see

the gold and take it from me."

"True, true," said Digit. "But that is why Allah sent it to this wilderness."

"I have an idea," Yusef said. "I will stay here until the basket fills with gold many times, and load the mules. Then I will hide the basket up in those rocks.

I can give the governor some gold, and come back for more whenever I need it."

"You are wise," said Digit. "It is a pleasure to find a man who is not so greedy that he forgets to think. That plan is good. Where are your mules?"

The merchant struck himself on the forehead and began to pull his beard. "What do I say! Fool, fool that I am! I sold my mules in the last village, where I bought this fine horse."

"Very well," Digit said. "I will stay with the basket, and with the gold. You ride your fine horse to the village and bring back mules."

"Oh, no," said the greedy Yusef. "I will stay with the basket. You take this money, and my fine horse, and go for the mules. But you must not tell anyone about the magic basket."

"Oh, I will tell no one," promised Digit. "But do not worry. Only a very stupid man would believe such a story from a little boy."

Yusef laughed. "That is true," he agreed. "No one would believe such a story. Go, and hurry back!"

Digit took the money from the merchant and climbed hand-over-hand up the horse's tail and onto the saddle. He looked down at Yusef and said, "I must tell you one other thing. You are new to the basket. If it does not bring gold on noon of the first day, just be patient. The gold is worth waiting for."

"Oh, I will be, I will be patient," Yusef promised. "There will be thousands of noons to come. The first one does not matter."

Digit left Yusef sitting there by the basket, waiting for the sun to reach the middle of the sky.

The horse was swift and strong, and by the time it was night Digit was at home. Before giving the horse to his mother, Digit let all his brothers look the horse over and ride it. But he would not tell them where he got the horse, or the money he showed them. Digit only said that he had sold many horses to get it. Then he gave the money and horse to his mother.

"Why do you giant fools never bring me money or horses?" the mother screamed at her huge sons. "You bring me nothing but trouble. If it were not for Digit, we would all starve." Her angry words made her sons very cross.

That night while the brothers filled the house with the rumble and thunder of their snoring, Digit crawled to the bed of his oldest brother and softly whispered, "I found the horses in the river where you threw me. There are many more there. In the morning, while the others still sleep, we will go there. When I whistle, it will be the signal to rise and go to the river."

Digit then crept to the bed of the next oldest brother and whispered, "I tell only you of this. I found the horses in the forest. Tomorrow we will go there. When I whistle, rise and follow me."

Digit told the next brother that the horses were from the mountain. To the next brother, Digit whispered that he had found the horses in the lake. He told the next brother that he had found the horses on the desert, and the next brother was told to follow Digit to the meadow. Finally, the last brother was told to follow Digit to a big cave.

While the brothers were sleeping, and dreaming of horses, Digit tied all their legs together.

In the morning, Digit gave a shrill whistle through a hollow tube. The brothers leaped up and began to run in seven different directions. Enraged, because they were tied together and were tripping all over, they began to hit and kick each other. Finally, they just beat each other senseless.

Digit said to his mother, "I am going after more horses."

"And where will you find them?" she asked.

"Wherever fools ride them," he replied.

And Digit went on looking for fools that could be tricked. And he found many. But you could say one thing about Digit, he was always good to his poor old mother.

Glossary

Abunawas (ah BOON ah wass), the name of a rascal-hero

Accra (ah KRAH), the capital of Ghana

Allah (AH lah), the Moslem name for God

Ato (AH toh), mister

Bandimba (bahn DEM bah), a people of the Congo

Darahi (dahr AH hee), a Moslem family name

Ethiopia (ee thee OH pee uh), a country in East Africa

Ghana (GAH nah), a country in West Africa

Haik (hayk), a lake

Hamdani (hahm DAH nee), a Moslem name

Injera (IN jeh rrah), a common food that looks like a large pancake

Kasilo (KAH see loh), the Spider

Kijipah (kee JEE pah), the Gazelle

Minu (mih NOO), "I don't understand," in the *Ga* language of Ghana

Mugassa (moh GAS uh), a deity

Mulugeta (moo loo GEH tah), an Ethiopian family name

Munz (muhnz), a small town in Ethiopia

Ndisah (nn dee SAH), the Spider's wife

Negus (NEH goos), an emperor

Sierra Leone (SEHR uh lee OHN), a country in West Africa

Uganda (yoo GAHN dah), a country in Central Africa

Wakaima (WAH kay mah), the Rabbit

Wanjovu (wahn JOH voo), the Elephant

Wizero (WAY zeh roh), missus

Wot (wut), a sauce made from chicken and served with injera

Yasu (YAH soo), an Ethiopian family name

Yemswitch (YEM swich), an Ethiopian family name

Yusef (YES eff), an Ethiopian name

Zanzibar (ZAN zih bahr), an island off the coast of East Africa

1 2 3 4 5 6 7—U—82 81 80 79 78